MW01110017

GOD
to
HIS
Daughters

A Thirty-day
Devotional
for Women

God to His Daughters
Copyright © 2015 Derrick L. Jackson

Unless otherwise identified, all Scripture quotations are taken from THE HOLY BIBLE, KING JAMES VERSION.

Published by TOWNSEND PRESS
Sunday School Publishing Board
330 Charlotte Avenue
Nashville, Tennessee 37201-1188

Printed in the United States of America

ISBN 978-0-9964797-1-4

To my deceased mother, the late Mary Bell Jackson-Stevenson; my beautiful wife, Laurie Lanakila Smith-Jackson; my lovely granddaughter, Sanai Marie; and the many strong and faithful women of Mississippi, Texas, and Tennessee who the Lord used at various stages of my life to help shape me into who I am and who I am becoming. Thank you for your love, support, patience, and wonderful investment in my life.

Also, to the "daughters of God" of First Baptist Church as a "salute" for Mother's Day and as a part of our yearlong celebration of 150 years of ministry. God has indeed favored First Baptist Church! Thank you for the wonderful privilege of allowing me to serve as your pastor.

Table of Contents

Introduction

The Bible speaks of the angels and elders around the throne of God crying, "Holy, Holy, Holy." Many have come to believe that the cry of "holy" is a natural response to a manifestation of who God is. God reveals Himself to His creation in a variety of ways.

The purpose of this thirty-day devotional is to provide women, "daughters of God," various ways to see and experience God for thirty straight days. Each short and practical devotion gives the daughters of God an opportunity to draw closer to God after meditating on thirty of the names of God referred to in Scripture.

The names of God are written in Hebrew or Greek forms with English interpretations. The reader will find scriptural verses at the beginning of each day's reading that serve as a source for meditation and reflection—with space to record personal thoughts for the day.

I pray that the daughters of God everywhere will fill their days with God and allow God to fill their lives with Himself. Utilize this devotion as a thirty-day supplemental source for renewal, refocus, and restoration.

For the Cause of Christ,

Derrick L. Jackson

Day 1

Abba

I AM YOUR FATHER

"Our Father which art in heaven."
(Matthew 6:9b, KJV)

The relationship between a daughter and her father may be difficult to express in words. She looks up to him as her hero, her protection, her standard of what her future husband should be, and so much more. To him, she is the apple of his eye, his pride, and his special joy. She is Daddy's little girl, no matter how much she grows or how far she goes.

Jesus refers to God as "Our Father which art in heaven." Jesus places God in the highest position, esteeming Him as the one to look up to. Not only is He above as One to hope in, but He is also in a position to see everything that concerns us. This knowledge of where God is gives us the blessed assurance of always being in His sight.

Jesus encourages us to see God as our Father, who watches over everything. He can see what we have need of, and He is able to meet those needs according to what He sees as best for us, according to His will. Our Father is also able to see when danger is present and protect us from all "hurt, harm, and danger."

What a loving Father He is! His love for you is unsearchable. In the eyes of your Father in heaven, there is no one like you. He would give the world for you. In fact, He has given more than the world because the world was not good enough for you. He gave Himself, and no good thing will He withhold from the ones He loves. You are His daughter, and He is your Abba Father, a bond that can never be broken.

Prayer

Father, I honor Your name. You are my Father, and I recognize that I am Your child. As my Father, I accept that You love me and You care for me. May Your love overwhelm all of who I am today; and because You love me, Abba, let me be all that I can be in You. May I find favor in Your sight and allow Your love to carry me throughout my day—guiding, protecting, and providing for me in every way. In Jesus' name I pray. Amen.

Personal Thought(s) for Today

_____
_____
_____
_____
_____
_____
_____
_____
_____
_____
_____
_____
_____
_____
_____
_____
_____
_____
_____
_____
_____
_____
_____
_____
_____
_____
_____
_____
_____

GOD TO HIS DAUGHTERS

Day 2

Jehovah Rohi

I AM YOUR SHEPHERD

"The LORD is my shepherd:
I shall not want."
(Psalm 23:1, KJV)

Genesis 29 records how Rachel, the daughter of Laban, was in the field tending her father's sheep. Her daily routine was to water the sheep. Apparently, there came a day when Rachel's life totally changed. Everything she did was normal up until that sunny afternoon. Rachel, who had always been a shepherd, now encountered the shepherd Jacob.

The question is not whether Rachel should have been a shepherd; rather, what is significant is that Rachel needed someone else to play the role of a shepherd in her life. And, if you study the relationship between Jacob and Rachel beginning in Genesis 29, you will discover that Jacob did for Rachel what she was not able to do for herself. He willingly took on her responsibilities as he cared for her like his own sheep.

The psalmist in Psalm 23 suggested that we have a shepherd far greater than Jacob. According to the psalmist, "The Lord is our shepherd." The Lord is *Jehovah Rohi*, who has the loving responsibility of caring for you, protecting you, and making sure that your every need is met. That's why the psalmist said, "The LORD is my shepherd; I shall not want."

Can you say that the Lord is your Shepherd? Are you able to lie down in green pastures? When you walk through the valley of the shadow of death, are you able to know that God is with you? Is your cup running over when you sit in the presence of your enemies? Does your head burn with the oil of His presence as goodness and mercy follow you every step of your way? Well, the Good Shepherd does these things for His sheep. He will lay down His life for you. Will you allow the Good Shepherd to shepherd you?

Prayer
Lord God, there are many things that are too hard for me and many roles that are very difficult for me to fulfill. I ask for Your help this day as my Good Shepherd. Bring me to a place of rest in You that I may receive restoration for my soul. In Jesus' name I pray. Amen.

Personal Thought (s) for Today

_____

_____

_____

_____

_____

_____

_____

_____

_____

_____

_____

_____

_____

_____

_____

_____

_____

_____

_____

_____

_____

_____

_____

_____

_____

Day 3

Alpha and Omega

I AM YOUR BEGINNING AND YOUR ENDING

"I am Alpha and Omega, the beginning and the end, the first and the last."
(Revelation 22:13, KJV)

When you look at a ring, you will see that it has no beginning and no end. Although there are rings that do have an opening, most rings are round and seem never-ending. For example, in looking at a wedding band, I have often wondered where the jeweler started and where the jeweler ended when making that ring.

God says He is the Beginning and He is the End, the First and the Last. He does not say that He has a beginning and He has an end. The reality is that God has no beginning, and He has no ending.

As His daughter, do you have a beginning? And if you do, you must have an end because the beginning cannot be unless there is an end. So when did you begin and when do you end? Did you begin in your mother's womb, or did you begin in your father's loins?

When you begin to see yourself as an offspring of God, born of His Spirit and His nature, you will then realize that He is your beginning and He is your end. This means that the spiritual part of who you are begins in God and likewise ends in God. He is, therefore, your *Alpha and Omega*. He decides your existence, purpose, and destiny. And, if you truly think about it, you will discover that what begins in God and what ends in God has no beginning and no ending. This is the secret of being born of an eternal Spirit and having eternal life. Remember that the beginning and the end are not events, but a Person.

Prayer

Dear God, I am learning that You are my Beginning and my End, the First of who I am and the Last of who I will be. Sometimes it seems difficult to understand all there is to know about me, but I thank You, God, that I can get to know me by getting to know You. Reveal Yourself to me more and more each day. In Jesus' name I pray. Amen.

Personal Thought (s) for Today

_____
_____
_____
_____
_____
_____
_____
_____
_____
_____
_____
_____
_____
_____
_____
_____
_____
_____
_____
_____
_____
_____
_____
_____
_____
_____
_____

Day 4

Emmanuel

I AM WITH YOU

"Behold, a virgin shall be with child, and shall bring forth a son, and they shall call his name Emmanuel, which being interpreted is, God with us."
(Matthew 1:23, KJV)

One of the fears that women have when considering their children is the fear of losing them. The loss can come in several ways, and the loss of a child is very difficult. Death has a way of robbing a mother of what she values most—her child or children.

Mary, the mother of Jesus, experienced the loss of her son in many ways. Yet, His name was Emmanuel. One might think that Mary should have never lost the one whom she called, "God with us." Actually, did she actually lose Him?

Emmanuel, "God with us," means exactly what it says. He is with us, and He is with you in this moment as you are reading this devotional. You may not see Him or feel Him, but He is there. Inside your heart is a witness that you are one spirit with God. You are not alone.

Every so often, He will remind you through His Word, saying, "I will never leave you or forsake you." When life becomes difficult, listen as He reassures you that, "When thou passest through the waters, I will be with thee; and through the rivers, they shall not overflow thee; when thou walkest through the fire, thou shall not be burned; neither shall the flame kindle upon thee" (Isaiah 43:2, KJV). Is there anything more comforting than knowing that your God is with you? Dear Daughter, this is one thing you do not have to fear losing. God will always be there for you.

Prayer

Emmanuel, forgive me for doubting Your presence in my life. Sometimes it's hard to see You when the situation seems overwhelming. I pray that You will strengthen my heart to know that I am never alone, and that I will never lose You or my place in You. In Jesus' name I pray. Amen.

Personal Thought (s) for Today

_____
_____
_____
_____
_____
_____
_____
_____
_____
_____
_____
_____
_____
_____
_____
_____
_____
_____
_____
_____
_____
_____
_____
_____
_____
_____

Day 5

Elohim

I AM YOUR CREATOR

*"In the beginning God created the
heaven and the earth. "*
(Genesis 1:1, KJV)

There is no record to prove the exact size of the universe, but we do know that it is enormous. Astrophysicists and other scientists continue to make discoveries of galaxies beyond galaxies. Notwithstanding, the argument remains as to how it all began. Was it really a big bang, or is there a magnificent Being called God who created it all?

Indeed, God is responsible for the fullness of the world we live in, and He is responsible for you. He is not some ordinary "god" far off somewhere, unreachable or unsearchable. On the contrary, He is

Elohim. Now imagine yourself in the hands of this God who has created all things. Considering that He holds all things in His hand, where are you in comparison to the heavens, the planets, the six billion-plus people alive today, the animals, the trees, the extraterrestrial beings, and all of life out there? You are in His hands.

You may wonder how a God so great can be concerned with someone as small as you. David asked in Psalm 8:4, "What is man, that thou art mindful of him? and the son of man, that thou visitest him?" David then said in Psalm 8:5, "For thou hast made him a little lower than the angels, and hast crowned him with glory and honour."

You are more to God than all of the greatness of creation. *Elohim*, the All-powerful Creator, knows you by name. And, He knows every detail about you. He is worthy to be called the God of all creation because He knows all of His creation precisely as He knows Himself. Thank God that the Creator knows you by name!

Prayer

Heavenly Father, it is easy to get lost in a world so filled with all that there is, but not with You. I thank You, Father, that You know me by name. You know my up-rising and my down-sitting, and You know me from the inside out. Carry me through this day and help me to be mindful that You are mindful of me. In Jesus' name I pray. Amen.

Personal Thought(s) for Today

_____
_____
_____
_____
_____
_____
_____
_____
_____
_____
_____
_____
_____
_____
_____
_____
_____
_____
_____
_____
_____
_____
_____
_____
_____
_____
_____
_____

Day 6

Jehovah Jireh

I AM YOUR PROVIDER

"Abraham called the name of that place Jehovah-Jireh: as it is said to this day, In the mount of the LORD it shall be seen."
(Genesis 22:14, KJV)

There is a story in the Bible about Elijah and the widow of Zarephath recorded in 1 Kings 17:7-16. According to the story, this unnamed woman was about to cook her last meal to feed herself and her son before dying. As far as she knew, their lives were over. She was helpless and had no one to call upon.

She had reached the end of her life and, apparently, she had concluded that it was the end of her son's life as well. Death surrounded her, and all hope was gone. Little did she realize that there was a God known as

Jehovah Jireh who had more than enough for herself and her son.

In Genesis 22:14, Abraham testified to the fact that God is a provider. Knowing neither *how* God would provide a sacrifice nor *when* God would provide a sacrifice, Abraham was assured in his heart that somehow and some way God would provide a sacrifice. Just as God provided for Abraham and for the widow of Zarephath, God will also provide for you.

It is easy to sing, "Jehovah Jireh, my provider" when all is well and your hopes are high. But the lyrics to the song become difficult to sing when you have run out of options and God does not seem to be anywhere in sight. It is in those times that God wants you to remember that He is your provider. He will give His angels charge over you because Jehovah Jireh cares for you. While sometimes He seemingly waits until the last minute to provide, He wants you to possess the blessed assurance that He is indeed your provider.

Prayer

Lord, thank You for sustaining me thus far. Thank You for providing for me and my family the way You have. I know that You see what I have need of and where I lack. I pray, God, that You meet all of my needs according to Your riches in glory. In Jesus' name I pray. Amen.

Personal Thought(s) for Today

_____
_____
_____
_____
_____
_____
_____
_____
_____
_____
_____
_____
_____
_____
_____
_____
_____
_____
_____
_____
_____
_____
_____
_____
_____
_____
_____
_____

Day 7

Ishi

I AM YOUR COMPANION

*"It shall be at that day, saith the LORD,
that thou shalt call me Ishi: and shalt call me
no more Baali."*

(Hosea 2:16, KJV).

One may wonder why God preferred to be called "Ishi" and not "Baali." Was it because other gods were referred to as Baali or Baal, and He wanted a name exclusively for Himself? Perhaps that could be part of the reason. However, consider for a moment that the word *Baali* refers to a husband as lord; it lacks forms of endearment, and it projects the concepts of fear and subjection. However, *Ishi*, while also referring to a husband, produces an affection of love. It engages the emotions and arouses affections. *Ishi* speaks of a love relationship between a husband and his wife.

When God reveals Himself, He does so based on how He chooses to manifest Himself in a particular situation or to a specific individual. He is love, and one of the highest expressions of love that humans can experience dwells within the institution of marriage between a man and a woman. Thus, God engages us on this level to help us better understand and relate to Him as a God of love and a God of companionship.

God does not want us to be fearful of Him, as might be evidenced in the relationship between a master and a servant. Oh no, God wants you to feel and to know Him as the true Husband of your life and all of who you are. He wants your relationship with Him to be built on an endearing love. Anything else would not be love, and consequently would be unacceptable to God. You are never alone with God in your life.

Prayer

Dear God, You are the lover of my soul. You have married me in love, and in this love I give my heart to You. Let me not wander after other gods and things that cannot satisfy. Let my heart be turned to You and You only. May You teach me how to love You and find true love in You. In Jesus' name I pray. Amen.

Personal Thought(s) for Today

Day 8

El Shalom

I AM YOUR PEACE

"The LORD said unto him, Peace be unto thee: fear not: thou shalt not die."
(Judges 6:23, KJV)

International news media outlets and world leaders are calling for peace in various parts of the world. Within the past few years, there have been wars and civil unrests far more than ever expected. Neither the United States nor the United Nations is able to uphold peace, and yet the world is thirsting for peace.

The dictionary defines the word *peace* as "freedom from disturbance, conflict behaviors, and the fear of violence." But Jesus had another definition of *peace* when He stated in John 14:27, "Peace I leave with you, my peace I give unto you: not as the world giveth, give I unto you. Let not your heart be troubled, neither let it be afraid."

What kind of peace was Jesus talking about, and why isn't the world experiencing this kind of peace? We must remember that Jesus is the Prince of Peace. However, His peace is for those who yield to His Lordship.

El Shalom means "Lord my Peace." It is this peace that the writer spoke of in Judges 6:23. It is an intimate spiritual flow of God's energy manifesting as peace within the spiritual life of a person who is focused and loyal to Him. When the peace of God is present, not only does it affect the spirit, but it also moves within the mind and floods the soul with the reassurance and rest that everything will be all right. God Himself becomes peace in a person's life, producing the freedom to live without fear of anything.

Prayer

Most Holy God in whom there is no shadow or form of darkness, search me and take away everything that disturbs my life. I pray, dear God, that You will give me Your peace today that my heart will not be troubled. Let Your peace, Jehovah Shalom, rule in my heart and be the umpire of my soul now and forevermore. In Jesus' name I pray. Amen.

Personal Thought(s) for Today

_____
_____
_____
_____
_____
_____
_____
_____
_____
_____
_____
_____
_____
_____
_____
_____
_____
_____
_____
_____
_____
_____
_____
_____
_____
_____
_____
_____

Day 9

Jehovah Rapha

I AM YOUR HEALER

"I will restore health unto thee, and I will heal thee of thy wounds, saith the LORD."
(Jeremiah 30:17a, KJV)

When Jesus went to the cross of Calvary, He paid the price and took away our sins and the sin of the world. In those deep dark hours of His death, He bore our sicknesses and diseases. Moreover, it clearly states in Isaiah 53:5 that "with his stripes we are healed."

God is concerned about the "wholeness" of our being. He referred to this wholeness in Jeremiah 30:17. He desires that your spirit be made whole, your mind renewed, and your body well. The same God who healed yesterday is also able to heal today. That is why He is *Jehovah Rapha*—God, your Healer.

There are many instances in the Bible where Jesus healed the sick. God has not stopped healing, whether it be spiritual healing, physical healing, mental healing, or personal healing. God desires that you be whole.

Are you whole today? Do you believe that Jesus is able to heal you and make you whole? Can God do for you what He did for persons in the past? Do not stop believing that God is your healer. Regardless of the length of time it takes for the physical manifestation, God will indeed heal you and make you whole.

Prayer

My God, I believe Your Word is true, and I know that what You said You are able to do. I pray, God, that the healing virtue of Jesus Christ heals my body and my mind. I also pray for someone who may be hurting at this moment and in dire need of Your touch. May the healing Balm of Gilead flow from the living streams of heaven into Your vessels today. In Jesus' name I pray. Amen.

Personal Thought(s) for Today

_____

_____

_____

_____

_____

Day 10

Jehovah Nissi

I AM YOUR BANNER WHO GOES BEFORE YOU

"Moses built an altar, and called the name of it Jehovah-nissi: For he said, Because the LORD hath sworn that the LORD will have war with Amalek from generation to generation."
(Exodus 17:15-16, KJV)

Moses, Joshua, David, and even Abraham fought wars in order to get to where God wanted them to be. The children of Israel endured defeats, but they celebrated many years of great triumphs. God was with them, and every time they lifted Him as their banner in obedience, they experienced a successful outcome.

God went before them, and He encamped round about them. As long as the people stayed true to their God, He stayed true to them. Amazingly, God was faithful to the people even when they were faithless and unfaithful.

God fought for them, and it was God who led them. He drove out the enemies from before them so that they could inhabit the Promised Land. What God did for Israel He will also do for you.

Jehovah Nissi is the Banner over you, waving in the face of the enemy that the battle has already been fought and the victory has already been won. So every time the enemy tries to make you believe that he is winning and gaining ground against you, remind yourself that there is a Banner over you and that Banner is the Lord. He goes before you. Your God will fight your battles. Let Him lead the way.

Prayer

I present myself to You, God, not as a victim but as a victor. When You defeated the enemy on the Cross, You defeated the enemy once and for all. Thank You, God, for destroying the works of darkness and giving me the victory that I need to make it through every day. Thank You for being the Banner over my life. In Jesus' name I pray. Amen.

Personal Thought(s) for Today

_____

_____

_____

_____

_____

_____

_____

_____

_____

_____

_____

_____

_____

_____

_____

_____

_____

_____

_____

_____

_____

_____

_____

_____

_____

_____

_____

_____

_____

_____

Day 11

Jehovah MiKadishkim

I AM YOUR SANCTIFIER

"Ye shall keep my statutes, and do them: I am the LORD which sanctify you."
(Leviticus 20:8, KJV)

In Leviticus 20, you will observe that God gave a command to be holy. There appears to be a contradiction between verse 7 and verse 8. In verse 7, the writer said, "Sanctify yourselves therefore, and be holy: for I am the LORD your God." However in verse 8, the writer says, "I am the LORD which sanctify you." The question is, who takes the lead in the sanctification process?

God takes that lead. God will never require anything from you that is impossible. In other words,

He knows that a person cannot sanctify himself or herself alone. Therefore, He makes provision, and He becomes the One who sanctifies. He takes the lead in the sanctification process.

If God does not sanctify us, then we will never be able to approach Him, or be the vessels He calls us to be. The shortcomings and sinfulness of the Adamic nature disqualify us from having communion and fellowship with Him. But because God desires to have a family and does not desire that any should perish, He becomes our sanctification.

Jehovah MiKadishkim, the Lord your Sanctifier, makes you holy and makes it possible for you to live a holy life. Your reaction to His command in verse 7 should be that of willing submission. With a response of submission, God is more than able and willing to sanctify you. Thank God that He is your Sanctifier!

Prayer

Dear God, in my flesh, I know that I fall short. Sanctify me, dear God. Forgive me of all my sins and cleanse me by the blood of Jesus. Help me to be a sanctified vessel desirable for Your use. I want to be more like You, and I want You to dwell in me in the fullness of who You are. In Jesus' name I pray. Amen.

Personal Thought (s) for Today

_____
_____
_____
_____
_____
_____
_____
_____
_____
_____
_____
_____
_____
_____
_____
_____
_____
_____
_____
_____
_____
_____
_____
_____
_____
_____
_____
_____

Day 12

El Shaddai

I AM YOUR STRENGTH AND SUFFICIENCY

"God said unto him, I am God Almighty: be fruitful and multiply: a nation and a company of nations shall be of thee, and kings shall come out of thy loins."
(Genesis 35:11, KJV).

El Shaddai means "Lord God Almighty" and the "All-sufficient One." This name also has a meaning that women can relate to more closely: "the All-breasted One." That is to say, He is the God who nourishes, supplies, and satisfies His people. Most often when we speak of breasts, the feminine characteristics of a woman come to mind, and one of the first pictures perceived is that of a mother nursing her child.

Does this mean that God is a woman or mother? In terms of spirituality and truth, God is Spirit, and there is neither male nor female. However, God does reveal His characteristics in masculine and feminine terms. In this disposition of who God is, He purposely projects His nature like that of a woman caring for her children. He desires you to know that He is the One in whom you can find nourishment, and He is sufficient to satisfy you as you grow and live in Him.

In this relationship between you and *El Shaddai*, the parental bond is manifested. It is in this state that you get to know the voice of your heavenly Father. Additionally, you learn that your dependency is of Him; and as you feed off His nature, you will experience that no one else can satisfy and nourish like Him.

It is because of His strength and His sufficiency that you can be fruitful and multiply in every area of your life. Thank God for His strength and His sufficiency in your life!

Prayer

Oh, what a joy it is to experience fruitful life in You, dear God! Like David, You satisfy my mouth with good things and all my days are numbered before You. What a privilege and an honor it is to be called Your own. Thank You, Father, for being my El Shaddai. In Jesus' name I pray. Amen.

Personal Thought (s) for Today

Day 13

Jehovah Tsidkenu

I AM YOUR RIGHTEOUSNESS

"In his days Judah shall be saved, and Israel shall dwell safely: and this [is] his name whereby he shall be called, THE LORD OUR RIGHTEOUSNESS."

(Jeremiah 23:6, KJV)

Have you ever had a day when you felt like you could never please God? Have you ever had a day when guilt seemingly "dogged" your every step? There are indeed things in life that do go wrong and mistakes in life that seem to never go away. By the time you think that it is all over and done with, another situation or person surfaces to remind you of what you did wrong. It gets worse when your conscience will not let go of what happened.

Unfortunately, we sometimes beat up on ourselves, feeling condemned and unworthy of God's love.

You might wonder if God ever forgave you. And if what you did was really magnified, you might feel as if He cannot forgive you. As a result, the old cliché "I am nothing but a filthy rag" becomes your new anthem. God reminded the persons of Judah that it was His righteousness that would allow them to make things right with Him. They did not have to walk in condemnation and guilt. God was making all things right with them.

Paul also understood the concept of righteousness. He wrote something very helpful in Romans 8:1, which reads, "There is therefore now no condemnation to them which are in Christ Jesus, who walk not after the flesh, but after the Spirit." Allow yourself to connect with the words, "no condemnation in Christ Jesus." *Jehovah Tsidkenu*, God my Righteousness, takes away all condemnation. So the next time the accuser tries to accuse you of something you know God has forgiven you of, simply say, "*Jehovah Tsidkenu*, God my Righteousness, has already taken care of that for me."

Prayer

Father, thank You for being my Righteousness. I thank You that You became sin that I may become righteous in You. I stand strong against every thought of condemnation and every form of guilt and shame. I plead the blood of Jesus over my life, and I thank You, Lord, that Your blood speaks for me. In Jesus' name I pray. Amen.

Personal Thought(s) for Today

_____

_____

_____

_____

_____

_____

_____

_____

_____

_____

_____

_____

_____

_____

_____

_____

_____

_____

_____

_____

_____

_____

_____

_____

_____

_____

_____

Day 14

Adonai

I AM YOUR LIMITLESS POSSIBILITIES

"Abram said, Lord GOD, what wilt thou give me, seeing I go childless…?"
(Genesis 15:2a, KJV)

Abram, who was later named Abraham, was a man of great wisdom. He understood that when dealing with this strange and unknown God he had to address the Deity rightfully. At this point in Abram's life, he did not have a covenant with this God but was willing to trust God, knowing that he had come too far to turn back.

Abram's desperation in believing what he was promised pushed him into a place where he had to address the impossible. And for him, he had no child and did not believe he could have one. Therefore, he began to reason with God based on God's sovereignty. In addressing God as *Adonai*, Abram appealed to the side of God that was able to make anything happen. Abram reasoned that if God were able to make him a father of many nations, then the least He could do was give Abram an heir.

Although the task was impossible in Abram's eyes, it was very possible in God's eyes. God in His Sovereignty is ultimate Power, Dominion, Rule, Supremacy, Influence, Authority, and all that there is. Nothing is impossible with Him because He exists in the realm of all possibilities. This is why Jesus said, "With God all things are possible" (Matthew 19:26). Name the impossible situation that you face today. In fact, list everything that is impossible for you and with you. Now present that list to God, and ask Him which situation or circumstance is impossible with Him.

Prayer

Most Sovereign God, You existed before all things; and before You there is nothing, and neither will there be anything after You. Father, as I think about how great You are, may You help me to believe that nothing that concerns me is impossible with You. Let my life be filled with limitless possibilities; for You are my God, and with You all things are possible. In Jesus' name I pray. Amen.

Personal Thought(s) for Today

Day 15

Rabboni

I AM YOUR MASTER TEACHER

"Jesus saith unto her, Mary. She turned herself, and saith unto him, Rabboni: which is to say, Master."
(John 20:16, KJV)

One of the first groups of people you meet in life is teachers. Prior to teachers, your parents and family members are the first people you experience in this world. Parents, family members, and teachers often teach you and influence you in different ways. Think about it. From your mother's womb to this point in your life, you have been taught and influenced by a variety of people. Can you think of that one person or group of persons who had the greatest influence upon your life? All of us have had teachers we loved, and others we hated or tolerated. However, some teachers stand out and occupy a special place in our hearts because of their influence in our lives. These persons often become "beloved" by us. We have another Teacher, however, who is the greatest teacher who has ever lived. Mary referred to Him as *Rabboni.*

When the Jews referred to someone as *rabboni,* they referred to that person as "master." The person received that title by being a unique, gifted, and masterful teacher. In other words, the teacher became so knowledgeable and authoritative on a topic that he became a master of it. Mary saw Jesus as "Master Teacher." She was transformed by His knowledge, authority, and compassion. As a result, she received forgiveness of her sins. For Mary, Jesus was Master of what He lived and said, and she valued that. Hence, at the grave, the voice she recognized was the voice of her Master because He had been her beloved Teacher.

God seeks to be your Teacher. He has given you the Holy Spirit to aid in the learning process. Will you allow the Spirit of *Rabboni* to teach you? First John 2:27 teaches that the Holy Spirit will indeed teach you. What do you need to learn today? Allow the Spirit of *Rabboni* to become your Master Teacher.

Prayer

Holy Spirit, You are the Great Teacher. You are my Rabboni. You are my Knowledge, Wisdom, Understanding, and Counsel. I desire to know You intimately and learn more of You. I submit myself as a student in this lifelong journey with You. In Jesus' name I pray. Amen.

Personal Thought(s) for Today

Day 16

Yahweh Sabaoth

I AM YOUR RULING HOST

"Then said David to the Philistine, Thou comest to me with a sword, and with a spear, and with a shield: but I come to thee in the name of the LORD of hosts, the God of the armies of Israel, whom thou hast defied."
(1 Samuel 17:45, KJV)

What an audacious remark made by David! Persons go to war with weapons and the latest armory fully prepared to face the enemy. What did David go with? A name? One would think that David was joking. No wonder the Philistine giant, Goliath, felt insulted. A name? Is that all you had, David? Saul was willing to give you his armor. What were you really depending on? David was a strange

GOD TO HIS DAUGHTERS

young man. He exercised his trust and made his boast in nothing else but a name. Interestingly, David did not depend on his name. He depended on the name of the Lord of hosts, *Yahweh Sabaoth*.

Capital One, a credit card company, has a question as part of its commercial that asks, "What's in your wallet?" Well, the question important to you today is, what's in your mouth? Are you like David, with a particular name you can mention when faced with the terror of your life? Or, are you depending on things that have no power?

God is the Lord of Hosts. That is, He is the One Ruling Principality over all the hosts of heaven: angels, stars, spirits, and every terrestrial and celestial being. All that is named must bow to His name. In His name is the power over every other name, and He has the power to destroy and bring down every form of the enemy. Your Father is *Yahweh Sabaoth*, the Lord of Hosts. Trust in His name.

Prayer

Father, I thank You because You are Yahweh Sabaoth, the Lord of Hosts. I commit my life to You today and all that I have I place in Your hand. I praise You for commanding Your angels concerning me that they keep watch over me to protect my going out and my coming in. I will not walk in fear because I have Yahweh Sabaoth watching over me. In Jesus' name I pray. Amen.

Personal Thought(s) for Today

_____

_____

_____

_____

_____

_____

_____

_____

_____

_____

_____

_____

_____

_____

_____

_____

_____

_____

_____

_____

_____

_____

_____

_____

_____

_____

_____

_____

Day 17

Jehovah Shammah

I AM YOUR LORD WHO IS ALWAYS "THERE"

"It was round about eighteen thousand measures: and the name of the city from that day shall be, The LORD is there."
(Ezekiel 48:35, KJV)

Today, as you are reading and meditating upon the Scripture above, picture yourself as the city of God and the temple of the Most High. Imagine all of the places you need to go today. Imagine also that there will be some who you do not know who will notice you as you arrive at your various places today. Upon your arrival, will they be able to observe you and say, "The Lord is there" because you are there?

Did you know that you are the temple of the Holy Spirit of God and that God dwells in you? *Jehovah Shammah*, meaning "the Lord is there," places a possession upon whatever or whoever that dwelling place is. God names His dwelling place for Himself and after Himself. *Jehovah Shammah* desires to shine through you.

In this manifestation of God as *Jehovah Shammah*, the focus turns toward the carrier of His presence—YOU. This is a glorious and magnificent honor, but it is also a huge responsibility.

Be mindful, therefore, of whether the next time someone looks at you he or she can see God in you. Is God there? You are the "glory carrier." Carry it well because "The Lord is there." Where? In you! God is always "there" in YOU.

Prayer

Heavenly Father, You are more than I can ever imagine or conceive. It is humbling to know that I am a carrier of You. What wonder it is to know that You are in me. May You cleanse and consecrate me as Your dwelling place, a holy habitation for You. May Your glory radiate from my life that those who see me might be influenced by Your presence in me. In Jesus' name I pray. Amen.

Personal Thought(s) for Today

_____

_____

_____

_____

_____

_____

_____

_____

_____

_____

_____

_____

_____

_____

_____

_____

_____

_____

_____

_____

_____

_____

_____

Day 18

El Kanna

I AM YOUR JEALOUS GOD

"God is jealous, and the LORD revengeth; the LORD revengeth, and is furious; the LORD will take vengeance on his adversaries, and he reserveth wrath for his enemies."
(Nahum 1:2, KJV)

Jealousy is an attribute that many persons possess at various stages of their lives. Some suggest that women are quicker to admit their jealousy than men are. Interestingly, some men, when asked, will never admit to being jealous.

There are some women who will ask their husbands or significant others whether they are jealous when it comes to them. If the men say yes, the women are secretly happy. However, if the men say no, the women are a little disturbed because they really want the men to be "just a little jealous" when it comes to them.

In today's devotion, you are meeting *El Kanna*, the jealous God. If God is jealous as He said He is, does it then make jealousy a good thing? In addition, since He is your Father, should you also be jealous concerning your loved ones? It must be understood that although God is making us in His likeness and image, there are certain attributes that we must learn to exhibit rightfully and with godly control and godly intent.

God's jealousy for you as His child and bride has no evil connotations with it. He expresses this aspect of who He is against the enemy. Thus, it works in your favor as an attribute of His love and manifestation of who He is, because He will fight on your behalf and do whatever it takes to protect you. No one touches the apple of God's eye—which is you—and neither can the enemy have you. Your God will not allow it. He is a jealous God.

Prayer

O Lord, how excellent is Your name in all the Earth! How loving is the sound of Your name, El Kanna, to my ears. Your love for me is unimaginable and Your thoughts toward me are absolutely good. Be jealous for me this day, O God, that I may see Your salvation as You conquer and destroy my adversaries. Thank You, Father, for loving me with Your jealous love. In Jesus' name I pray. Amen.

Personal Thought(s) for Today

Day 19

Yeshua

I AM YOUR SALVATION

"She shall bring forth a son, and thou shalt call his name JESUS: for he shall save his people from their sins"
(Matthew 1:21, KJV)

In many cultures and traditions, the naming ceremony of a child is highly recognized and celebrated. In these cultures, the naming of a child carries generational and eternal significance. In other cultures, the naming of a child is based upon family members, important events, or various pronunciations. Have you ever thought to yourself, "What's in a name?"

The name *Yeshua* is the Hebrew name of God's person for salvation. In English, Christians and others translate the word *Yeshua* as "Savior" or "Jesus." *Yeshua* means "God saves," and that is exactly what Jesus does.

The name *Jesus,* or *Yeshua,* has become the name above every other name. It is the most recognized name in the whole Earth and within all of spirituality. What Jesus was "called" or "named" had both eternal and earthly significance.

The lesson for today is to be careful what you "call" or "name" persons, events, or circumstances. What we call ourselves and others has great significance in terms of who we and others become. So what's in a name? Everything. Do not allow yourself to be called what you do not want to manifest. However, do remember what you have in Jesus. You have salvation. He is *Yeshua*, your salvation!

Prayer

Lord, I give You praise for who You are, and I bless Your holy name. Search me, O God, and know my heart today. Search me and show me where I have become a name that You have not called me to become. Teach me how to name those things that are dear to my heart—my family, my vision, and the works of my hands. May everything that concerns me bring You glory and honor. Thank You for being my Salvation. In Jesus' name I pray. Amen.

Personal Thought(s) for Today

Day 20

Paraklētos

I AM YOUR COMFORTER AND COUNSELOR

"The Comforter, which is the Holy Ghost, whom the Father will send in my name, he shall teach you all things, and bring all things to your remembrance, whatsoever I have said unto you."
(John 14:26, KJV)

The most important person on Earth today is the Holy Spirit. The Holy Spirit is not a thing or a feeling, but a person. The Holy Spirit is God. The Holy Spirit is the Spirit of Jesus Christ. Just as each human being has a spirit, so the Holy Spirit is the Spirit of the Deity we worship as God.

The *Paraklētos*, which is Greek for "Holy Spirit,"

can take on many forms or manifestations. When Jesus first introduced the Holy Spirit in the book of John, He referred to Him as the Comforter, Counselor, and the Spirit of Truth. The Holy Spirit is also described in other places in Scripture as the Breath of God, the Seven Spirits of God, the Standby, and our Helper.

The Holy Spirit is the Enabler, the Anointing, and the Presence of God. He gets the job done. He is the One who gives us the ability to accomplish the work of God. He is the One who draws us to Jesus. He is the One who gives us the ability to call Jesus our Lord. The Holy Spirit is also the One who is in you and is working on you to become matured in God.

He feels your hurts. He sees everything you go through. Moreover, He intercedes on your behalf. You may never see Him, but He is always there. He speaks even when you are not listening. He is the Friend who sticks closer than a brother. This is why He is the *Paraklētos* or Paraclete, because He is right there by your side, willing and ready to help you in your time of need.

Prayer

Holy Spirit, You are the Spirit of Jesus and the Spirit of my Father. I recognize Your presence in my life. I give God praise that I am born of You. My life would have been nothing, void and empty, without You. I pray that You will draw me to You in deeper intimacy. Let me know You as I am known of You. In Jesus' name I pray. Amen.

Personal Thought(s) for Today

_____

_____

_____

_____

_____

_____

_____

_____

_____

_____

_____

_____

_____

_____

_____

_____

_____

_____

_____

_____

_____

_____

_____

_____

_____

_____

_____

GOD TO HIS DAUGHTERS

Day 21

YHVH

I AM YOUR EVERY NEED

"God said unto Moses, I AM THAT I AM: and he said, Thus shalt thou say unto the children of Israel, I AM hath sent me unto you."
(Exodus 3:14, KJV)

Some scholars believe that Hebrew is the language God chose to use when He first made covenant with humanity after the fall of Adam. It was within the communication of this language that He introduced Himself by name. No other language carries so much power in its pronunciation than the native tongue of Israel.

It is of value to note that the most sacred name for

God consists of four letters—*YHVH*, pronounced as "Yod-Hey-Vav-Hey" and interpreted as "Yahweh" or "Jehovah." It means, "I Am That I Am" or "I Am Who I Am." What a way to introduce oneself!

No other description or name comprises all that can be, other than "I Am." Perhaps Moses was confused when he first heard the name. However, God knew that the children of Israel would indeed recognize Him by that name because God had a "track record" with the children of Israel.

This name of God was so revered that it was forbidden for anyone to utter the sound of it. With this name, God reminds us that He desires a personal and active relationship with His people. Thus, when God speaks of Himself as the I Am, He is saying that "I can be all that I need to be for you." Aren't you glad that your God is your every need?

Prayer

Lord, I will lift up my eyes to the hills from whence cometh my help because I know my help comes from the Great I Am. You did not bring me this far, God, to leave me, and neither did You build Your home in me to move away. I need You this day more than I have ever needed You before. You are my every need. I worship You, God, for who You are, and I reverence Your holy name. In Jesus' name I pray. Amen.

Personal Thought (s) for Today

_____

_____

_____

_____

_____

_____

_____

_____

_____

_____

_____

_____

_____

_____

_____

_____

_____

_____

_____

_____

_____

_____

_____

_____

_____

_____

Day 22

Shophet

I AM YOUR JUSTICE

"Grudge not one against another, brethren, lest ye be condemned: behold, the judge standeth before the door."

(James 5:9, KJV)

Have you realized that in life it is easier to pass judgment when you are not the one on trial? Isn't it interesting that some tend to always know what the outcome should be or should have been when they are not the ones in a particular situation? It is like watching a game and observing how the players are moving back and forth, trying to win. You are not the one playing, but you sure do have an opinion of how possible it is or could have been to win.

Is there anyone who has not been guilty in the eyes of God? Was there ever a time you, for example, were perfect?

Paul, in the book of Romans, wrote that "all have sinned, and fall short of God's glory." So, then, who has the ability to judge? James taught that we should not hold grudges against another or attempt to judge another. According to James, God is the only rightful judge.

The reference to God as *Shophet* means that God is the "Righteous Judge." He judges righteously and with all fairness. His judgment is not biased or lacking in anything. He sees the end even before the beginning starts. Interestingly, when He judges, He makes provisions for the guilty to become innocent. He takes no pleasure in unjust scales and balances. He defends the poor and speaks for the voiceless. He ensures that everyone has an equal playing field so that when He judges His judgment is sure. Is He therefore not worthy to be our Judge? Of course He is! Who is worthy to sit in the seat of judgment and declare justice? Let's give to God the honor that is due His name. Let us leave judgment and vengeance to the One who is able to judge, the Lord *Shophet*. He is your justice.

Prayer

Lord, my place is in You, based on Your grace toward me. I do not attempt to ascend to Your throne as Judge, and neither do I try to usurp any authority over and above You. If I have failed in any way by passing judgment when I should not have, forgive me. Guard my heart that pride and self-righteousness will have no place in me. In Jesus' name I pray. Amen.

Personal Thought(s) for Today

Day 23

El Gabore

I AM YOUR MIGHTY GOD

"The mighty God, even the LORD, hath spoken, and called the earth from the rising of the sun unto the going down thereof."
(Psalm 50:1, KJV)

Might is the ability, power, or force to do something. Many people desire to do things but lack the capability. There are weaknesses, limitations, and even circumstances that could also explain why one may not be able to accomplish what he or she desires to do. This is, however, not the case with God.

El Gabore, the Mighty God, is exactly who God is. There is nothing that God desires to do that He cannot do. God is so mighty that His Word alone is able to accomplish His will. This is what is called real power. Everything about God's abilities has sufficient power to perform as desired. Thus, we cannot speak of might without speaking of power. His Word, as mentioned earlier, has power. His presence has power. His name has power. His Spirit has power. His characteristics have power. In fact, God is so mighty in power that we reverence Him as the Mighty God and Omnipotent One.

Who wants a powerless and weak god? The reason for honoring and depending on a deity lies within that deity's ability and might. The more the deity performs victoriously, the more the deity receives praise and worship. The more the deity conquers and dominates through might, the greater the deity is feared and reverenced. Have you observed Jehovah's record of accomplishments? Fortunately for you, you have a God who is in a class all by Himself. There is no other deity that can be compared to Him. Your God is *El Gabore*, the Mighty God. Just a word from Him will change everything. Hence, if He has given you His Word, stand on it and believe it because it has the power to work wonders in your life.

Prayer

Father, forgive me if I have underestimated who You are and what You can do. Forgive me for doubting and not fully believing that You can do what You have said. You are not a God who is unable to deliver. You are my *Mighty God. In Jesus' name I pray. Amen.*

Personal Thought(s) for Today

_____
_____
_____
_____
_____
_____
_____
_____
_____
_____
_____
_____
_____
_____
_____
_____
_____
_____
_____
_____
_____
_____
_____
_____
_____
_____
_____
_____

Day 24

Jehovah Chayil

I AM YOUR WEALTH

"Naomi had a kinsman of her husband's, a mighty man of wealth, of the family of Elimelech; and his name was Boaz."
(Ruth 2:1, KJV)

One would think that Ruth was a very lucky girl to get Boaz as a husband. After all, he was rich, single, and presumably good-looking. Not only that, he was a well-respected and influential man. Ruth had nothing working in her favor as far as she was concerned. Her husband had died and she was a foreigner. She had no skills, no children, no money, and nowhere to go. To make matters worse, Moabites were not allowed in the congregation of the Israelites.

Sometimes in life it only takes one thing to make the difference. There are times when no amount of contacts, beauty, money, brains, or anything else can help when the fulfillment of destiny requires only one particular thing. All you need in this life is the favor of God. And, when it is time for favor to manifest, it will change you from a peasant to a distributor of wealth.

Boaz did not give Ruth his wealth when he encountered her. He only allowed her to partake of the leftovers in the field. It was Ruth's encounter with *Jehovah Chayil* in the secret place that gave her access to Boaz's wealth.

She had placed her trust in the God of Naomi, her mother-in-law. This God was also the God of Boaz. Ruth would never have had access and ownership to the wealth bestowed upon Boaz without first having met the God of that wealth. When you encounter God as *Jehovah Chayil*, the God of Wealth, He gives you access to wealth because He confers unprecedented favor that cannot be denied.

Prayer

Lord, I lift up my voice to You today, crying out for Your favor. It is not only favor with man that I ask for, but favor with You, O God. Jehovah Chayil, my God of Wealth, bestow upon me Your spirit to prosper in all that I do and all that I set my heart to. In Jesus' name I pray. Amen.

Personal Thought(s) for Today

GOD TO HIS DAUGHTERS

Day 25

Esh Oklah

I AM YOUR CONSUMING FIRE

"Understand therefore this day, that the LORD thy God is he which goeth over before thee: as a consuming fire he shall destroy them, and he shall bring them down before thy face: so shalt thou drive them out, and destroy them quickly, as the LORD hath said unto thee."
(Deuteronomy 9:3, KJV)

One of the most remarkable features of God is that of a consuming fire. He is either a consuming fire or the refiner's fire. To the enemy, He is always the consuming fire. But to the ones He loves—like you, His child—He becomes the refiner's fire.

When God expresses His love, it often burns like fire, and one can literally feel the burn. The sense of fire is not to destroy or to punish. Its purpose is to scorch out impurities in order to purify the vessel. Is it painful at times? Yes, but the end result is worth every touch of heat.

In today's devotion, you see God as the consuming fire, *Esh Oklah*. One aspect of love is to protect. Another aspect is to remove all impediments in the way of love. As it was in the case of the children of Israel, so it is with you.

In order to have the children of Israel possess the land, God had to drive out the enemy. Likewise, for you to inhabit your inheritance, God must destroy the enemy that stands before you. So He displays His love for you by manifesting Himself as a consuming fire against your enemies.

Prayer

Plead my cause, Lord, with those who have strife with me. As the consuming fire, destroy my enemies, seen and unseen. Let everything that stands against my progress in You be destroyed. Surround me with Your fire this day, O God, that I may become untouchable in the realm of the spirit. In Jesus' name I pray. Amen.

Personal Thought(s) for Today

_____
_____
_____
_____
_____
_____
_____
_____
_____
_____
_____
_____
_____
_____
_____
_____
_____
_____
_____
_____
_____
_____
_____
_____
_____
_____
_____
_____
_____

Day 26

Yahweh Tsur

I AM YOUR ROCK

"Blessed be the LORD my strength, which teacheth my hands to war, and my fingers to fight."
(Psalm 144:1, KJV)

In the book of Matthew, Jesus gave an illustration of a wise builder. He spoke of one individual who built his house on sand and another individual who built his house upon a rock. As is common with nature, there were rain, floods, and winds that demonstrated their power against those houses. It was just a matter of time before the strength of their foundations was made known.

It does not take a genius to figure out that the house built upon the rock would be the one left standing. One should always remember that the most important part of the house is the foundation. Likewise, the most important part of any life is its foundation.

The psalmist in Psalm 144:1 realized that inasmuch as God wants to beautify you and give you a life full of eternal bliss, He will not neglect your foundation. Without your foundation sternly fixed, you will never be able to withstand the things that naturally come against your life as a child of God.

As is common in how God works, He can trust no other foundation but Himself. God must be your God in and for all things. So as you think of God today, call Him *Yahweh Tsur*, the Lord your Rock. He is indeed your foundation.

Prayer

Dear God, You are the Rock of my Salvation, the One in whom I put my trust. Upon You, God, my hope is built and my future secured. I place my confidence in You and You alone. In Jesus' name I pray. Amen.

Personal Thought(s) for Today

Day 27

El Olam

I AM YOUR ETERNITY

"The LORD is the true God, he is the living God, and an everlasting king."
(Jeremiah 10:10a, KJV)

There are two types of deaths. One type is physical death—when the physical body becomes lifeless. The other type is spiritual death—which is a separation from God. The latter can be in effect while the former appears to be alive. In other words, a person can be alive physically and dead spiritually.

Many have asked whether there is life after death—that is, death of the physical body. Some have spoken of "near-death experiences," in which the person either experienced a pleasant side called heaven or a terrifying side called hell. As Christians, we believe that accepting

Jesus Christ as Lord and Savior secures an eternal life after death, full of heavenly glory. We all will live eternally somewhere. The penetrating question is, Where will you spend eternity?

Your journey into eternity is a journey that only you can take. No one else can take that journey for you. Hopefully, you have secured your eternal future in God. And if not, you can ask Jesus into your heart at this very moment, and He will give you eternal life. Eternal life is God. Not only does God state His name as eternal life, but also, Jesus (in John 17:3) provides proof of God as eternal life. He states that, "And this is life eternal, that they might know thee the only true God, and Jesus Christ, whom thou hast sent."

Beloved, eternal life is not just a state of being. Eternal life is the person of God, *El Olam*. Jeremiah referred to Him as the "living eternal God." Therefore, if you have God, you have eternal life, and if you have eternal life, you most definitely have God.

Prayer

Thank You, God, for opening my eyes to see that accepting Jesus as Lord and Savior is not just a ticket to heaven and an escape route from hell. Rather, it is the acceptance of God in my life and the ability to be in Him eternally. Thank You for being my eternal King. In Jesus' name I pray. Amen.

Personal Thought(s) for Today

_____
_____
_____
_____
_____
_____
_____
_____
_____
_____
_____
_____
_____
_____
_____
_____
_____
_____
_____
_____
_____
_____
_____
_____
_____
_____
_____
_____

Day 28

Ruach Elohim

I AM YOUR BREATH

"The Spirit of God hath made me, and the breath of the Almighty hath given me life."
(Job 33:4, KJV)

Ruach Elohim means "Breath of God." The Spirit of the Mighty One who is your Father and your God is more than you can imagine. In knowing who God is, understand that He is Spirit. Now, what is a spirit? A *spirit* is a force, energy, wind, air, or even the nonphysical part of a person. A spirit is invisible to the human eye because it lacks all aspects of physicality.

You may feel the effects of a spirit, but it is very difficult to capture a spirit in terms of formation or tangibility. Thus, the spiritual dimension where spirits dwell is quite different from the physical dimension where our physical senses operate.

God revealed a powerful truth when He said through Paul in Colossians 1:16 that "all things were created by him and for him." He is the One who holds all things in His hands. This is intriguing, because when one thinks of things he or she relates them to that which is physical, although there are spiritual things as well. Thus, God, being Spirit, is able to produce and work with that which is both physical and spiritual.

The *Ruach Elohim*, the "Breath of God," is the spiritual force or energy of who God is that creates and sustains. Job suggested that it was this *Ruach Elohim* who made him. God is the life behind all that exists, and if He separates Himself from any aspect of His creation, that part ceases to exist. Without Him there can be no life, because He is the *Ruach Elohim*. He is the breath behind everything that is created.

Prayer

Spirit of the living God, breathe upon me. In You I live, I move, and I have my being. You give me life. Indeed, You are my life. You have made me, and any good that I do will be because You have breathed upon me. Thank You, dear God, for the breath of life. In Jesus' name I pray. Amen.

Personal Thought(s) for Today

GOD TO HIS DAUGHTERS

Day 29

Ebed Yahweh

I AM YOUR SPECIAL SERVANT

"Behold my servant, whom I uphold: mine elect, in whom my soul delighteth: I have put my spirit upon him: he shall bring forth judgment to the Gentiles."
(Isaiah 42:1, KJV)

In the kingdom of God, the way to greatness is through service. Your heavenly Father makes it clear that the way up is down. Some people in this world's system act as though the one on the top in society is the "boss" or "master" whose duty is to lord that authority, rank, and position over others—but that is not the way in the kingdom of God. In God's system, masters are servants, and servants are masters who serve. If you can learn this lesson, it will be one of the most valuable lessons in your life in becoming all that God wants you to become. God used His Son as the "Pattern Son" to reveal this truth to us.

Many of the people who surrounded Jesus during His days on Earth wanted Him to be King. After all, He had power to perform miracles. He was influential, and He was the Son of God. However, His way of doing things was quite different from what His followers expected. Therefore, it became His responsibility to show His disciples how to be the "greater one." He showed them how to be the "greater one" by becoming the "lesser one." He washed their feet as a servant would his master.

Jesus understood that the greatest place of all is the place of being the *Ebed Yahweh*, which is God in servant form. As a result, God exalted Him and gave Him a name above every other name. Remember that your greatness lies in your service and your willingness to serve. It is easy to serve because you have a Special Servant who will help you.

Prayer

My Father and my God, Your ways are higher than my ways and Your thoughts are higher than mine. You have commanded that the mind of Christ be in me that I may think and act like You. Lord, You have no problem with my being great, and I desire to be great. But may my greatness come from a place of service and the willingness to walk in humble obedience to Your Word. In Jesus' name I pray. Amen.

Personal Thought(s) for Today

_____
_____
_____
_____
_____
_____
_____
_____
_____
_____
_____
_____
_____
_____
_____
_____
_____
_____
_____
_____
_____
_____
_____
_____
_____
_____
_____
_____

Day 30

El Channun

I AM YOUR MERCY

"The LORD God prepared a gourd, and made it to come up over Jonah, that it might be a shadow over his head, to deliver him from his grief. So Jonah was exceeding glad of the gourd."
(Jonah 4:6, KJV)

To understand the above verse, you will need to read the story of Jonah to learn of how he got to this point. He was grateful and appreciated the shade in which he found comfort. He could now experience joy and benefit from the tree that he did not plant or make grow. On this particular morning he found a tree full of shade available for his use. Prior to this, however,

Jonah had wanted to die and he wanted the people of Nineveh punished. He could not see the need for God to forgive them by showing mercy. As far as he was concerned, they deserved nothing else but the wrath of God.

If God had dealt with Jonah the way in which Jonah wanted to deal with the people of Nineveh, Jonah would have died. Yes, he was a prophet of God, and he did deliver God's message eventually; but, when it came to God's mercy and grace, he was no different from the ones to whom he had preached.

El Channun, the gracious God or the God of grace, has not dealt with you and all of humanity as deserved. Rather, He has demonstrated His mercy by not giving to you what is due you according to the consequences of your sins. He is gracious to you by giving you what you do not deserve and are not worthy of. But because He is your mercy, you experience "new mercies" every day. These new mercies come from *El Channun*, the gracious God. Receive and bestow grace today.

Prayer

My dear God, thank You for the abundance of Your grace. Your mercy has kept me, and Your grace has provided for me. May I remember Your grace and be gracious like You as I deal with others. In Jesus' name I pray. Amen.

Personal Thought(s) for Today

_____
_____
_____
_____
_____
_____
_____
_____
_____
_____
_____
_____
_____
_____
_____
_____
_____
_____
_____
_____
_____
_____
_____
_____
_____
_____
_____